Driving to Biloxi

Driving to Biloxi

poems by Edgar Simmons

LOUISIANA STATE UNIVERSITY PRESS Baton Rouge

Some of these poems have appeared in the *Yale Review*, *Harvard Advocate*, *New Republic*, *Prairie Schooner*, *Southern Poetry Review*, *Western Humanities Review*, *Antioch Review*, *Chicago Review*, *Massachusetts Review*, *Georgia Review*, *Motive*, *Sage*, *Trace*, *Silo*, *Janus*, *American Weave*, *Nova*, *Perspective*, *Descant*, *Impetus*, the *Christian Science Monitor*, the New York *Herald Tribune*, and the New York *Times*.

Copyright © 1968 *by*
LOUISIANA STATE UNIVERSITY PRESS

LIBRARY OF CONGRESS CATALOG CARD NUMBER: 68–8943

Manufactured in the United States of America by
HERITAGE PRINTERS, INC., CHARLOTTE, NORTH CAROLINA

Designed by Robert L. Nance

to my family
in England and America

Contents

Driving to Biloxi

Driving to Biloxi

Driving to Biloxi
the swamps and tarred roads and
rail ties hovering with the heat
myself suspended
with the yellow butterflies
over the swamp tracks

knowing these fiery rails will break
anytime now
into green
dusty faced ferns
& shell roads whistling towards the water.

Impressions

When I was a child I gave a burning glance
To a footprint framed down in clay,
To the splayed sand tracks along the hot beach.
The outline of a leaf, skeleton of a fish
Each elaborated sweet against the globe—
Clocked me right out of time.

And tales told against the darkness
Were impressed with dusk and swallow twitter sky
Till the very birds danced upon the sill
And all kings and statues of kings
Were with me and held my hand.

Letter with No Title

dear son:

when you left us you left
gazebos, heat and buzzards,
a gravelled febrile Eden
for the city.

won't you, like poor Cowper,
write us receipt of your mother's picture out of Memphis?
did you ever see her knit under a moon?
do you recollect
the bled dread blood drops are hers?
can you remember barefoot
how here with us you once
struck a living hi and ho
come bang a letter from the savage blue.
I wade my poems, the salt in my eyes,
I glare around for the boy not there.
he is in the tiger ruins or rambling ancient skies.
how can I climb that slick steeple
lean from it, crying aloud new mountain sounds?
did you have a rotten journey of it?
And how was the war?
We are well there is no news.
Dad.

Unpublished Reflections by Machiavelli

I take up what I need
At the time I need it.
For that reason I shall study ethics
When I am infirm.

I know a woman
Who wears rings and is spirited
And when I leave her room
I pass a window where a man at his prayers
Slants his fingertips together—
He is blind
His praying hands not a steeple
But the poles of a cross

                      —I am about to

Understand this—
I shall burn this reflection
Smacking of general benefit.

Keats' Trodden Weed

I have given my life
And bloom now in a marriage
Following of course many ragged days
And much stony updrifting
Night voyagings underground
In later times my tongue stuck out hungry at the sun
My lisping mouth cut and caressed
A weed is but a hungering wait
—The lowing heifer first hit me
Brought me to an old low friend, the mud
Where I was hospitably detained
As intricate breed mixed with wedding
With piping flutes
The bride's foot upon me
Her instep high and warm and teeming
Now his anxious stride flattening and blinding
Moulding me to the consummate moment
With him, with her, with pipes, with mud, with sun.
Let me tell you I would not trade my part for any.
I was brought up to bear the proof of their fire.

Wind at the Eve

We cannot act
Without moving toward a phantom:
See Keats spy his bird
And Plato draw cave for cave;
Each grand enfold
Falls like speckled joy
Within the webbing time and space,
The matrix where zooms
The hurrying bone, hare-fast and hungry.

And there are requests:
Distill, my Lord, said the turtle
And He did
And the fox asked for elusive leaps,
The deer for a quick twitch of horns under moon,
But myth, eyeing galaxies, took a menacing grip and sighed.

We rattle the world for our babies,
Sob, shrug, are baffled by the dead—
That one, too, is under wraps,
Is energy in a sheeting wind
Which crisps the phantoms
Spooled along the stairwell
And, drawn down the oblique roof,
Shrieks "Alive! Alive!"
In goodly eve talk.

Rousseau at Neufchâtel

Let not dissension clutter the afternoon:
Nothing more chilling than the fracas
Of leaves barreling down limbs to bud.
Or were there a runnel outside my window
I could view its mad wee pace, abide its
Stormy teapot babbling and all sounds of scrambled nature
Conjugating, adding, and subtracting; all brittle
Concatenations which brew a right good hoarfrost,
Stretch a rabbit ear or consummate a March noon:
Such dissonance is the natural chant and rant of wisdom
Blessing the man and the room that it enters.
But keep out on this wiry afternoon obstinate men.
I would be beguiled if only my ear could hear
The fine ratchety gnawings, the pond's burp and bubble,
The satin quiet snappings of beak and petal,
The crunch, mist, powder, and honeycomb:
Nature's cozy fisticuffs that but romance the heart.
Admit not this day any chill splinter of spleen.

Leonardo's Notebooks

the rain is
making children
rocks are rolling
down the mountains
to be their bones
winds gather
warm breath
the soil
washes round
to flesh them
the oceans flood
tart
blood to veins
—come down, come down
the rain is
making children.

The Sea Harp's Spray

For James Laughlin

In the beginning you are dark sayings
In the sea harp's spray

Moved by narcosis
Whirled like an eye

—Wired and vesseled
As any musk or oyster
You ruminate asthmatically

Your eyes traced with snakes
Their coilings strumming in your brain
Flashing the long ache
In incipiency
The ache in the crooks and folds
Of awareness

—You are the dark sayings in the harp's
Saturate spray
—The crystal honeycombs
And webs that spread like hieroglyphs
To make your mouth
Glitter with the sea's bright peelings—

Winding and turning
In a black like olives
The torsion comes,
The holy screw,
The yellow hairs of your head spinning toward the beach.

Dylan Thomas in Indiana

The great giant is dead. Dylan dead.
Sheltered from a Paris rain I read a yellow handbill
On a bookstore window lighted by streetlight flames—

And the widow and the flaxen children
Will be grateful for anything at all . . .

And I remember first he pinched a lady's bottom
In Indiana moonlight while a party—liquidly literary—
Spored, whorled in the woodsy cabin.
Afterwards he humped his elbows on a camper's table
And gazing through screenwire on a backporch
Saw corn growing under an Indiana moon.

We chattered over the rough boards a radio script,
The crinkle-haired poet bombing with me
Bad, made-up lines across the table.
Resonant beyond belief he became
Southern planter, Negro slave running away, was a
Chicago gangster as I sweated more American grotesques
To feed all hot his ravenous maw—
Corn all around and upstairs the lady
In a maiden's pout swore and swore—
I remember her words to our giant,
"The rest of them treat you like God.
I'll be damned if I will."

And now in night of Parisian rain and flickering flame
I see my own eyes in the glass, my lips twisting out
The words that Death, a holy maiden pouting,
Had irrevocably etched
Like acid eating
Like white snakes coiling
Across the kinky head and pulpy pied face of Dylan
"The rest of them treat you like God.
I'll be damned if I will."

A Southerner's Lament for Lincoln

We can never love you completely
Because as hero you are marred:
A red crust, an aging rust glisters,
"Fratricide."

Yet you are the honest human symbol—
Rural, poor, and riding history's most homemade boat
Storm-tossed above the red running river
That split the head, the chest,
The stomach of the land.

You are the true Christian's hero
For he finds in your face as in Christ's
(And then in his)
The pain of suffering.

We feel strange joys
In loving you,
Our bearded, statued, quasi-friend.
You are
The beautiful razor rock
That cuts our sides
And we cry like frightened
Burnt-cork Hindus, "O, God,
Yours is the blood that cuts."

Blonde Majorette:
Close-up of Her Face on TV

Frown now   up at sun
take from sky   your flying baton.

The squirrely   freckles   on your face
are small suns   whose meaning baffles me
for I understand   only your love-frown to sun

—this wheeling   freely slaving you—.

In your total commitment   to that matter in the sky
you cannot be ever masking, masking:
Voilà! Exposé complêt.
O pretty kitten   you are bitten
like sugar fed to eyes
rich plums in the glandstream.

Your vulnerable concert   like snake charmer
lion tamer   sun shooter   beauty tragedienne
just misses   vulgarity.

Your act of concentration   (later fit for passion)
shows—

For this honesty I thank   your fear of public embarrassment
should you miss
your   my   the world's   baton.

Early Passion in a Puritan World

I remember a story of my youth,
a whitewashed Thursday afternoon with
pale green lemon yellow lights flickering on and off
in the dusty, straw-backed railroad car, and my hands
finding a strange, unbelievably large, enveloping and
weirdly ennervating world of sex in one
girl
not buxom but sufficient
to altogether portray the very far side of
floating worlds in greens and yellows, of
pitch blackness; a girl sufficient for
Lethean voyage where peril and joy were
limitless. We strangely rocked in the dark roll and
whistle of a train bound mother safe, past
the gravel roads, riding its own severe track down
to New Orleans and the anticlimax of Mardi Gras.

This was the band trip and every pew in every
church was blown out of the window as if an
exhilarant pagan typhoon had washed the very clay
crust off the protestant south.

Varsity Rag

thirteen and running out of his Christian yard
to a gramophone across two fields
he swam with the music through the weeds
to a fluid girl in a summer house
going round in a green dancing gown.

she took him and marched him to the music
her warm breath saying I am Virginia
one of the adopted daughters—who are you?
but he stuttered and said play it again
and tight against her
went round in a latticed sun
playing at propinquity.

out of his dark winey dream
she was saying here is my sister
come to the ball

and it was not her alone who came
but her gown
her powdered face
her ornaments at ear, at ankle, at wrist
her hips forged like sweet hysteric melons
from the string of waist
she was all fluff and flux
working on him like the sea

his hands and feet parrying all Eden
—everything suffused him
her red hair
her breast's riddling sharps and rounds
until he knew heaven's unions
and the separations of Hell—

she was saying I am Claudette
and he bent his brown puddle eyes to the floor
where her silver pencil heels
spoke like an axe

now in a chorus around him they were crying
you must come tomorrow
Helen comes home from College.

—numb on his own steps, his body folded,
fingers trailing in the dust
he took his milk and three vanilla wafers
the feathery blood
searching
spinning maidens
out of reach.

Music from a Southern Town

Scene at Christmas time
a white grocery   in a Negro section of Natchez
run   charged   hollered and whipped by
a high-piled charactry blonde   cerise slacks   red blouse
mother of 2   who dimples to me   with her rose ceramic nails
the telephone
                    and I listen to a jazz recording
cut by me and 2 Negroes   across the river in a sloven town.

Perhaps the whole thing got too Negrofied   for this world
(I knew a fellow so Jewish   it wasn't even funny)
climbing the yellow clay hill to fetch from covers   a freckled
liver-spotted   ninety-pound Negro drummer,
refuse of funeral parades   beer parlors   and night work
sassing drums in white clubs   flung over floodland, La.

High on that mustard bank I saw dust light   pouring
under the oyster wood house   leaning on cinnamon sticks
then he & I picked up the harmonica man   and crossed
the silver bridge to La.   two drums and one mouth organ
crying the Southern story.
                    One more drum   and it would have been fit.

Inbetween the dinky crater-gray   beer dumps
The Colored King of Record Makers   made his Machine for Recording
scratch and zoom and holler   up the little dusty
police-patrolled street.

We cut a record   then another
and on the third   to the huffing harp
I read To Be or Not To Be.

Now in the grocery   I amplify   the reeds and soggy drums
over the blonde's fine speaker
bass drum and tinkling tambourine   bulging like Christmas bells
our music swimming   in the store's   faked and elegant frost
lighting up the blonde's   piled up hair   & sounding next door
in the tavern's brown drowsy fumes   buzzing like home
in a dark worker's ear.
                    We have funeral songs
                    we have visceral blues
                    we have romps of resurrection
everything fogged as thunder   and blaring now
out on the Christmas street
                         jazzbone licks
                         stumbling pangs
                         sprung rhythms
                         webs of lush dark

Christmas illuminations   growling over the phone
the death of taboo.
                    We have Southern Fireworks
                    for a Southern Christmas
                    we have foe-kin friends
                    gamboling in song
the verboten record played over a telephone
roaring onto the street
through coils   of unseminal electronics
hot december's fireflies batting the screen
myself standing before a wheaty Kellog's display
with that awful reineddown blonde in red.
                                    jazzbone licks
                                    stumbling fireworks—

When the mad begin to dance
what tender wrack
what dust from stages.

Revere Beach, Boston

He had never seen water cut such a figure
On the form of the land as the waves on Boston;
Nor heard such a mighty rush of sound pound the land
As that afternoon on a concrete Boston beach.

Alone he had ridden, a streetcar and then a bus,
Walked between the ping and mouse-gray steel
Until he saw and heard the sound of the sea
Biting like the spiked-teeth bucket of a crane.

He urged the pounding jar itself in his mind
In place of her, who, on another strand,
In another time, could not say what was wrong,
Could not do their love the compliment of naming its enigma.
He remembered in her eyes the mystery of love wounded,
Love staring, of love creeping away.

The sea pounded over the thought of her,
Shoved him now in gaudy darkness to the trill
Of the carnival's yellow dancing tent
Ballooned along the Boston asphalt shore:
Now the cropping tide sounded dimly in the distance.

Later, on bus and streetcar, her voice returned
Hung in the iron silhouette of the still city,
Trumpeted darkly its weak, ignoble query.

Baseball: 0 for 2

The Mets are my companions in New York:
Ensconced on a leather bar seat I
Forget the raffish roar of sidewalk heat
Pummeling now silently behind me
Against the tavern's blank glass eye.

I cling to the dark leather horseshoe
My hand curled around the beaded glass:
Anchor against return to a drab cage
Slung high in the metropolitan upstone
   Where for two years now
   her ceremonial girdle
   —erstwhile household badge
   lies on the floor, its larder keys
   splayed there under dust.
So I thank them—the silent Mets,
The cameramen, the engineers,
The Beerblade sponsor, the barman
And the efficient machine on the wall
Projecting through the dark
The soft pads of light.

Journey to Headland

I sit with my Irish cat, sleepy at the hearth.
I have been pubbed and cottaged
And now the hairy peat is fired.

Ninety paces from Yeats' golf shack
My feet against this stone floor
I am like this headland thinly plunged to sea,
Driven to ditch my past.

It is late and we are tired
But Rosses' cockled shore inclines me to its circles
Where a dark cemetery I find,
And climb and lie down
Graves at my feet and head
And stars and bulls around me—
I see the Celtic crosses lock horns with the sleeping bulls
And on my back I read their stone filigrees on the sky
(There is fractious figuring all night
The eye of language is at school).

Across the bay, dark Benbulben
Escapes—a mountain rising,
A purple needle leaving dark links below.
  I go home and stroke my cat
  Her sleepy mouth opens wide.

An American Abroad

comes up to cathedrals slow
dawdling like a child in the lap of a sleepy maid
his eyes in her choirs and transepts
his body slumbering in the spin of apses
as if a penny grace and the long world
spun in a child's sun forever;

in Hants he moves cool and blind over the nave graves—
Jane Austen and Izaak Walton
dead in the sleeping belly of the church
rich in stone light, hung in time
like this cloister in twilight
where cowled men sweep past him
twirling their fringed bell cords
blown along in their passion sandals
—egg round in beige robes they descend;

nine miles out of Cork he sees a castle's ruins
—vines and stones trapped in a slow tumbling frieze
into the River Lee; he seeks among the ruins,
bends to the mould, the mud,
the undressing that must be,
and knowing he might never return
he drinks from every village cup

its chain tying him to horizons,
stabilizing his feet in dusk;

often he is drunk with the sun in public squares
slightly bronzed and leaning forward
himself purchased and wrapped.

Begin and End with
Water Music in Ireland

The thirteen had said Come anytime to tea and
I rowed to the island at the haying time,
seeing them run in from the fields like wind-up toys
and in the kitchen under damp thatched roof
sudden there was salad, tea, and whispering grace:
flaxen haired the noon save the children now in dark lash demur.

Later, for my convenience, herself led me
to a dark bedroom where clothes hung everywhere to dry:
under a bed a tall white chamberpot and
there with but two geese in a corner I relieved myself of liquid
and then herself came in and I walked with her
and she so holy swilled it out to sea
and I, caught still as in a thunder,
remembered childhood and the night swack of dishwater
dashed from the back screen to invisible night grass,
remembered all our holy liquids, our blood and bile,
our waters and the clownish tumbling excretions
of our souls' hot heavens—these and the juices of our Adam's apples
and the fountains that lace the stars and pulse the rabbit's ear;
now at the bay's edge, herself staring out to time beyond time,
I remembered the ferry and father's strident
horn honk
high above on the midnight levee
Wait! Wait!

the dark ripples scintillant now
under the descending carlights
merged now to the rock of rubber tires on ferry planks,
then flap-lap—the churn depths paddle our tired bottoms fondly:
what geese in flannel sky with warmer homing cry?
what gladder water music than all the holy liquids spilled to love?
And we on this island, at the edge of spinning seas,
felt underfoot no whirling, no drowning
and there had been none in the seas of mother wombs:
no distressed powers these waters
but capable, even unto final rock.

World of Child Drummers

in my zeal and showoffness
as a child drummer I would
drown out my father's mandolin

and he would shrink his merry tinklings until Columbia the Gem of the Ocean

sounded only in
his joking smile
that tried to tell me something of the way he
always had to
disappear
into the threadbare suit of his living
in order to make
me slick Jack,

saying, "It's a poor family that can't afford one dude,"

and yet he
was begging
for a chance to play.

Halloween Story

I

I went out to my father's grave
And, knowing his sense of humor,
Said "Boo!" on Halloween.
Even the daisies laughed
And what a sweet snort
From the old oak himself.

II

My old Aunt Sarah will vouch for this:
She sat sharp jawed in the Ford
At this scene of several lunacies.
Then she laughed big as a mule
And strode over the gravelled road and together
We watered the flowers, pinched the weeds.
Somewhere a gay way off
Witch jays wove blue eights
Among the cherub stones.

Waking the Mind

Job said
God undermined me
to make me
better by a chain
of revolting understandings.

The form
of that dung hill
became for me
the foetus
of abstraction.

After a long time staring
I saw rising from it
fishes of delight
the lord growing.

Child at the Riverbed
(an anatomy of metaphor)

the child's beads

Metaphor's cousins are

the images of button bushes
in water, all reflections,
sights in fog, in haze and at
twilight or around a curve,
the closed door that bursts open,
"Surprise!" a wink, a squint,
a glance aslant; grottoes, echoes,
images in dust, theatre stages,
impersonations, vibrations,
pulsations, statues, paintings,
silhouettes, impressions in wax
and sand and clay, rhythm and rime,
shows, shadows, hedges, fringes,
gowns themselves and all this in

a scheme of relatedness
things in layers, comforters
and quilts, rain on the
glass, dreams and screened
porches, all angles, umbrage,
the whole meteorological face
of the humidities wheezing

the shutter eye, the fourth
dimension, the sixth sense:
an infinite number
of eyes
to see
for
you:

"In winter when the earth is covered
with snow and ice—ah reflection—
I walk upon the sky."—Thoreau

This is all we need know of death.

reality and appearance: the former
living only in the latter, ice and
snow writing new legends upon the
world as does lattice, lace, yolks,
jokes, Jonah in the whale, all
parables, myths, blessings, prayers,
players, passwords, rites, dice, and
games, all correspondences, including
letters, mementoes, memories, mottoes,
charms, initials, hearts slashed white
against the trees, parasols and pulp,
the gods that failed—idols in moon-

light awash and adream, any forest
we run against at night, in likeness
we seek, in unlikeness, that which

> is canny and kinky, all
> duplicity and puzzles, rugs and
> wheels, proportions and intervals,
> all undulations and analyses,
> analogies, exorcism and magic,
> vertigo and levitation, hooks and
> eyes, buttons and zippers, ropes
> and ladders, mines and caves,
> squatting and the labyrinthine
> manner of the mind in its act of
> reflexion: acceleration, conden-
> sation, regression, survivance.
> To cut out paperdolls is childish
> but not to men who have gone to pieces.
> The artist squints and blinks:

Thoreau—"A day of low mist in the
woods may be counted on to be a good
day for observation since the confined
view compels the attention to near objects."

—Such as the family.

catalysts, syntheses, all
transcendence, manichaeism,
the pendulum's action and
reaction, river demons and
nightmares, fallen angels,
spirits of lakes and springs
and wells, malevolent ghosts,
masks, tropes, ruins, tombs,
deserts, revelations, reveries,
whispers, codes, rain dances:

"Error comes from exclusion."—Pascal

II

the spirit reflexive

Man himself is metaphor in his spiritual reflexion
The penetration of the self by the self
The spirit grasping itself by means of itself
Returning entirely upon itself
This it is to become self-conscious:

A billion births, a billion billion births
Vast universal-diverse
Life's imitations for survival forced
Into skull session in the gray gymnasium

The borning machine within the borning machine
Gestation in insulation
While the snows of time
Lash outside the yellow windows of the mind.
Inside us the child-spirit grown alchemist;
Things in him rise and turn
He receives and suffers
Discerns and divines
Reflexive feeds on the precipice of pause
Plies his fictive rays.
Thinks matter.
This is the primordial relation
Lone bitter-sweet intimacy
'Twixt creativity and form—
Forked passion in the sky:
Thought and matter oiled and locked.

III

the child at the riverbed

Thought, jeweled eyeball, crowns the forehead
Of the web-winged *daemon* child who,
Like a giant lighted chameleon,
Scours the dark windy lofts,
Plunges diviningly to find and seize

The ancient riverbed,
To swallow with his passionate eyes
The secret face of the ancient absolute riverbed:
Here is the place of secret meeting and meaning
In and beyond our lives:
Here the child-spirit at its source—
Womb foreign to formulae
In secret acts of invisceration
Infinitizes the self by
Descending to the roots of being
And reimmersing itself in dreams.
The child-spirit performs the ritual of brooding gestation,
In quiet ecstasy steams new myth,
Sizzles free will,
Bears a child,
Exorcises death in acts of integrality
So that there is no unfathering man, no woman without child.
In the ancient riverbed of life and death
The child sleeps and dreams
Old and new meaning into
Old and new beings
And who has seen the child
Has seen God the father
And who has been the child
Is safe in his arms.

Implication as Absolute

How say we do not attain it
Because we do not lay hand on it?
Is not distance, is not separation
A span as real and true as steel?
How deny metaphor this fleshing?

Curtains garnish us with the squint of appraisal,
Gives the heart the necessary space
Between itself and stage.
Curtains and the space before it
Give us a focus we can believe.

Because a drum major's baton
Is more often apart from him than part of him
Is it not the more factual in those
Blank instants it is away from him?

It is at distances that we learn love,
At distances that we sense perfection,
That we see it shimmer. A space
Allows a shimmer; how else would we
See heat waves, but at a distance?

They cannot dance else.
This is the distant dance of metaphor,
Real because it is the bough out of reach.
This is why Romeo loves Juliet and not Romeo.
The only queen
Is the queen out of reach.

Talking Through Chaucer's Hat

Dear John Crowe Ransom:
I have posted a package to you.
If I were to tell you—as I do—
This was Chaucer's hat
You would believe me out of love.

How can this hat mean but to me alone
Unless I declare it Chaucer's—and not my father's at all?
Make what you will of the hat—
Headgear for your scarecrows
But mainly you must send of yours
Some sweet toy in the blood
That declares man's head to the skies
That announces with eccentric myrrh
Our divining brotherhood.

As for the hat
Throw cards in it during rains
Let your grandsons play robbers
For it is at once the most mortal immortal thing I own.
My father's mind sweated it in the sun
He lifted it for ladies, and sat beside it in church.
My mother brushed it, my sister crushed it.
It is an awfully human hat. As a love does it disturb you?
It must pleasure you as a joke more human than divine.

Of course it is, finally, Chaucer's hat
And you may in your entrance hall so label it
For the old dust of man is on it
The ancient unblinkable unbreakable
Sign.
—Brush it—the dust will return
And ever frail light will crown it.

Babbit Rabbit and Thematic Turtle

"Indeed, the little world is the imitation
of our ancient paradise, when we inhabited it in innocence."

—John Crowe Ransom
in "Humanism at Chicago"

the bunch-backed turtle

The stones chill, ague the web
Sun glare nips the nose
But always glass greenly mirrored
In his watery eyes, the finish line:
The reeds of swamp, quiet sylvan stockade
Secretly his in a time out of mind;
These and the voyagings among blue stones, ruby birds
Are the visions that deploy, mindless, the feet.

the denotufted rabbit

Shook out of sight
Is the rabbit's jiggle of scene.
His boggley bound,
His plash footed romp,
Fogs all essence and attar of life.

The Main Fact about a Hill

The main fact about a hill
is that it stands up.
This is a blessing,
a girl with flowers
announcing a song.

The song is without end
which tells us of the girl,
reminds us again that
the main fact about a hill
is that it stands up.

Did I say the girl carried flowers?

The Art of Brother Keeping

the instant you can
accept the colon
you are christened
in the right compromise

that no things are alike
but are related.

the greatest
the necessary
the most powerful leap of metaphor
is when I decide
I am you

    the result is
a birth
a
metaphysical differentiation
carried out and on
not in flesh but in spirit—
prophetic fact in time
more than children of our flesh.

At the Seed and Feed

Carrying his mandolin in the curve of the afternoon
Past the hot and shaded porch
Past flead dogs and the kings of bottletop checkers
Shooting their crowed eyes beyond their strawbrimmed hats
I followed my father into the dark of an old store.

Among men and tin and bottle goods
Among bonneted ladies with crochet hoops
White tambourines etched with blue flowers
We stood in Jesus-sweet gloom.

Now Father's wizard mandolin sings the store alive
The strings lightly throbbing,
Tinkling on and on, the frets marking his fleshy fingers
His notes like plums in the dark.

Soon a fox yelps down the evening
And cows loll home spearing from a covert of trees;
Now the piney church turns yellow for Wednesday prayers
And Father, slipping the pick under the mandolin strings, bows

Dwindling in the sun.

Bow Down to Stutterers

The stutterer's hesitation
Is a procrastinate crackle,
Redress to hot force,
Flight from ancient flame.

The bow, the handclasp, the sign of the cross
Say, "Sh-sh-sheathe the savage sword!"

If there is greatness in sacrifice
Lay on me the blue stigmata of saints;
Let me not fly to kill in unthought.

Prufrock has been maligned.
And Hamlet should have waived revenge,
Walked with Ophelia domestic corridors
Absorbing the tick, the bothersome twitch.

Let me stutter with the non-objective painters
Let my stars cool to bare lighted civilities.

Blue Colophon

If eternity exists
Shall we not, out of the fact of it,
Rise out of it, emerge from our death
Through shale and the scrolls of shells and
Bark and from the wind's cavities in sea rocks.
(For that will I gladly sleep forever—less one.)
Does not apostolic mean unending
And is a conifer not the shadow of the long time
(There could never be collusion about such trees).
Why can I not read smoke, air streams, or the clouded calligraphs?
O for a colloquy with God on these matters hearing him say,
Just here, just there, just this or that is the clue,
Hearing, Dread not, Eden is the unending book,
Eternity its stigmata, its justifying sign,
Its hooded, its blooded, its blue colophon.

The Magnetic Field

Distance . . . which by definition
Indicates a separation from self
Is the healing poultice of metaphor,
Is the night-lighting of poetry.
As we allot to elements their weights
So to metaphor we need assign the
Weight of the ghost of distance.
Stars are stars to us
Because of distance: it is in the
Nothingness which clings us them
That we glory, tremble, and bow.
O what weight and glory lie abalance
In the stretch of vacant fields:
Metaphor, the hymn and hum of separation.

York River Land

Flat land, unperturbed by hillocks
Such as mine, grass to the bay's edge:
Not a tempest in your day's blue dream.

Through the years I have visited you
And nothing ever raises you
Thin, level, grass-soft spit of land
Content as if time were concrete.

And yet, to the gull, frog, and katydid
I know you offer problems:
You feed and starve them
Freeze and burn them in the
Silence of clipped sedge
Yellowing always into the glass blue sea.

Today I project my being into the wet depths of you—
Flat blade and rapier round grass
Spiking in the bending wind—

The sea's wringlets
Lave my wrists
And this affection
Comes and goes.

Sons of Sad Dreams

The night of the storm my smallest boy
Woke out of a damaging dream
And, finding with blind small hands
The hall's walls and finally my bed
Crawled in between the sheets.
"I don't want to die,"
He whispered hot against my back.
I turned and rubbed his head.
"I want to sleep with you,"
And I thought,
O sad,
You will
And rocked him
Held him not too fierce.

A Note to Walt Whitman

When they say,
When you begin to say,
He has had it,
He has slumbered through it,

Rise and shake the coarse long hair
And lumber, no matter stiffly,
Through May woods.
Bathe in the cold stream,
Dry yourself on leaves,
Shake the tree vines
Until birds rustle and
The very woods resound
A rough and readied presence.

Return and write of
The bark on the hand,
The cold stream and the May bud;
Let birds scream, but not too shrilly,
Record the face's lines
And the muscle in the thick calf.

Faulkner

I

Having often gone privately
through woods and swamp lands near Oxford,
having often trailed in at night through his mother's parlor
in dirty duck pants and muddy sneakers, furtively bobbing
to aunts and spinster librarians lifting in the light
warm muffins —with sweat on him going past
the parlor lamp, going privately and steadily to his room
his heart topsy turvy
with pine pitch & Negroes in the boiling sun—
the shrieking birds, the slick coon hounds
resounding in his blood
inveigling in him a grand privacy

such good hostelry often repeated and privately magnified
the elements breaking and burning
beginning a pattern
the words finally lighting him
like the sun lighting the courthouse in Oxford.

II

—Days and nights of spidery calligraphy, exquisite as a monk's,
jesus corporals gliding from his pen—
Faulkner's private
hot line, his mammy, nanny, his fine rockabye,

his fingers funding the vast rubble of time, the hiss of controls
working, his face slightly swaying & downed with a lichen that
fringes the slowly turning turret of his face,
the carp-like threads of the thrusting face in a lean to the paper—
he is the ecstatic fox running under the Pleiades,
moustache bristling like a toucan, moist lips making vowels
of agreement—mind, fingers & face dancing so as not to fall,
lips asserting private zonal priorities over the old
irrational cry: Faulkner assimilating Adam and his tree
branching the apples of vision, becoming the grease and shine
of amplitude, providing beneath the jelly
red horns   red cloven feet

                            wearing finally only the figleaf
of language, knowing that to have moved at all
was to have begun this necessitous rattley dance
this silent private flit through the plot of old thorns:

bard, scop, skald, trouvère
                       this slight Celtic minstrel
—this Falconer—armored—tussling with his bird.

Pegasus and the Prince

Where the sea meets the ploughed land
With only flat yellow sand between
I took my young son and set us there.
Edging the clodded field, a stand of pine
With woodsmen's chips as thin bright as dawn;
A turtle, feeling the sun on his hopscotch back,
Paced our thoughts through the low wild buttercups.
A clattering like a deer upbreaking a wooded hill
Proved only a woodchuck giantly fat and full of loud feet.
A crane on yellow-boned legs splintered against the sedge;
A curlew and a gull wound their big lonely clocks,
Vigorous chalk sticks drawing on the sky.
The baby, fretted by cones and clods, eyed me for a ride.
Now on my shoulders he rode, a prince,
Proudly reigning over cranes and chucks and chips
In the saddle of his always winged horse.

Song of the Moth

it is your sweet propinquity
spins my pinions
to you,
lovely light.
you I prefer
to the black dog scampering in dusk and stubble
bound to ground

for your shapely cone
shines its riddling fugue
of life and death
           —like brass distractions
           at an open grave—
and I touch and let you pander,
be my blending mean

my flaming trope
singeing me
teaching me
fiery hosannahs beyond the mouthing clay.

tell me I reach you to rise
and rise
in your white throb
and tell me
longing was not Faust's ruin
and tell me
in your sacral scathing
the holy ghost is pinched to life.